BLACK WOMEN ADULT COLORING BOOK

CELEBRATING THE BEAUTY OF AFRICAN AMERICAN WOMEN

THIS BOOK BELONGS TO:

PRESENTED BY TEAM DESTRESS

TEAM DESTRESS

DE-STRESS AND CELEBRATE THE BEAUTY OF AFRICAN AMERICAN WOMEN.

PLEASE SHARE WITH US YOUR COLORED PAGES BY TAGGING US ON INSTAGRAM

@TEAMDESTRESS

YOU CAN ALSO SCAN THE QR CODE BELOW TO ACCESS ALL OF OUR LINKS.

THE PAGES ON THE LEFT IN THIS BOOK HAVE INTENTIONALLY

BEEN LEFT BLANK TO PREVENT BLEED.